JULI FURTADO

JULI FURTADO
RUGGED RACER

Morgan Hughes

Lerner Publications Company ● Minneapolis

For my fellow road (and dirt) warrior, T. K., whose enthusiasm and encouragement got me back in the saddle after too many years.

This book is available in two editions:
Library binding by Lerner Publications Company
Soft cover by First Avenue Editions, 1998
241 First Avenue North, Minneapolis, Minnesota 55401

Website address: www.lernerbooks.com

Library of Congress Cataloging-in-Publication Data

Hughes, Morgan, 1957–
    Julie Furtado : rugged racer / Morgan Hughes.
        p.   cm.
    Includes bibliographical references (p.) and index.
    ISBN 0–8225–3656–0 (hc : alk. paper). — ISBN 0–8225–9812–4 (pbk.
: alk. paper)
    1. Furtado, Juli, 1967– —Juvenile literature. 2. Cyclists—
United States—Biography—Juvenile literature. 3. Women cyclists—
United States—Biography—Juvenile literature. 4. All terrain
cycling—Juvenile liturature. I. Title.
GV1051.F87H85 1998
796.6'2'092—dc21
[B]   97–29487

Manufactured in the United States of America
1 2 3 4 5 6 – JR – 04 03 02 01 00 99

Contents

Juli and rivals begin the first Olympic mountain bike race.

Climbing Mount Olympus

Under a cloudless southern sky, more than 40,000 spectators gathered at the International Horse Park in Conyers, Georgia, 25 miles from Atlanta, on July 30, 1996. As the noon sun scorched the dry ground, 29 of the world's best women **cross-country** mountain bike racers edged nervously to the starting line. In a few moments, they would begin the first women's Olympic mountain bike competition.

At the front of the pack, with No. 28 pinned to her handlebars and a miniature U.S. flag sewn onto her riding jersey, Juli Furtado waited. Juli was the best woman mountain biker in the United States—and perhaps the world. She had already won five cross-country national championships and three World Cup titles. She was hoping to add an Olympic gold medal to her trophy case. Juli had dreamed of this moment—competing in the Olympics—since she was a little girl.

"This is an incredible opportunity," she said before the race began, but added: "It's like any other race. Whoever wins is just having a better day." On this day, Juli was hoping to have her best day.

In this first Olympic race, as in many of her races, Juli's main competition was expected to be Canadian Alison Sydor. After months of training, Juli was confident. "I don't want to medal [finish second or third],"she stated. "I want to win."

The Olympic race course was 19.8 miles long. The riders would make three laps around a difficult 6.6-mile loop. The terrain was varied and difficult.

In cross-country mountain biking, racers hurtle over fallen logs and climb up steep trails covered with rocks and loose gravel. They careen down rutted paths at speeds of up to 40 miles an hour. They have to ride between trees and often the path is just wide enough for their handlebars to pass through.

Mountain bikers not only have to be strong enough to pedal nonstop, they must also be skilled in the technical parts of racing. They must be able to steer their expensive, high-tech racing bikes over a treacherous and unforgiving obstacle course.

As a former **downhill** ski racer, Juli had plenty of experience with high speeds and danger. Her attitude has always been, "The slower you go, the easier it is to crash." On this historic day, Juli hoped to take advantage of her reputation for attacking with speed.

Alison Sydor, with No. 3 pinned on her mountain bike, leads
Juli (No. 28) and others over the Olympic course.

Juli struggles in the humid heat of Atlanta.

She was not going to let up, not with an Olympic gold medal at stake.

Throughout the morning and into the early afternoon, the temperature had crawled up and up and up, finally settling into the 90s. Aside from the terrible heat and the rugged terrain, the layout of the race course would challenge Juli. Several days before the

Olympic race, Juli told reporters that the course's design wasn't ideal for her style of racing. Still, as the dominant American woman in this sport, Juli was expected to win.

"It's a really bad course for me," she said. "I'm much better on long climbs. This is just a bunch of short climbs. I don't have a lot of **anaerobic** power [the kind sprinters usually possess]. So, for me, it's going to be a really hard course. Maybe it would be better if I wasn't the favorite," she said.

When the race began, the best riders quickly set a fast pace. Soon, the most gifted and well-conditioned riders separated themselves from the pack. During the first lap around the 6.6-mile course, a group of a dozen racers formed at the front.

As expected, Juli and her rival, Alison Sydor, were at the front of the lead pack for much of the first lap. Experts watching from the sidelines agreed that Juli was handling the technical parts of the course—the winding, twisting **slalom** sections—more smoothly than was Sydor. But Sydor seemed to have more power. Juli was struggling on the fast, steep climbs, as she had predicted she would.

Juli's friend and teammate, Susan DeMattei, had just barely made the two-woman U. S. team by winning in the very last qualifying race. But soon DeMattei passed Juli. As she pedaled past Juli, DeMattei asked her how she was feeling. "When she asked me that," Juli said after the race, "I couldn't even answer. But I remember thinking, 'Sheesh, isn't the heat getting to you?'"

As the race went on, the gap between Juli and the leaders grew. Instead of turning her pedals with a smooth, powerful rhythm, Juli coasted whenever she could, hoping to save her energy for the finish.

Race day was one of the hottest days of the Olympic Games. Olympic officials sprayed the fans with cooling mists blasted from the high, arching fountain of a fire hose. Although Juli drank as much water as she could, it became clear that this wasn't her day.

After two laps, Paolo Pezzo from Italy was leading the race. She was nearly three and a half minutes ahead of Juli. Sydor was in second place. Juli continued to drop back. Although parched by the sun, she kept fighting.

As the field of racers spread out, fans saw that no one would catch Pezzo or Sydor. Juli's teammate, Susan DeMattei, was able to jump into third place and won the bronze medal. Juli finished in 10th-place, nearly eight minutes behind Pezzo.

"I just couldn't deal with the heat," Juli said after the race. "The heat just killed me. I tried to come back, but I just about had heatstroke. I'm really disappointed. I think my fitness was good. My legs felt great. But after the first lap, I thought I was going to explode from the heat."

Huge electric fans blew a cool mist onto the racers and spectators during the hot Georgia day.

U.S. Olympic coach Chris Charmichael tries to comfort Juli after her disappointing finish at the Olympics.

After her disappointment at the Olympics, Juli returned briefly to the professional race circuit. She had dominated those races in the past, but this year her performances did not get better.

In October, the manager of Team GT, the professional team Juli races for, explained why. Team GT's Doug Martin said that Juli had injured her left knee. He said that she'd raced poorly because she had been racing with a damaged knee. Juli hadn't told anyone because she hadn't wanted to use her injury as an excuse.

Juli had major surgery to rebuild the knee. Doctors transplanted the healthy **anterior cruciate ligament** of a donor into her knee. Then, they replaced her damaged cartilage with cartilage that had been grown in a laboratory.

Sounds like science fiction, doesn't it? Juli says she had the scary operation because doctors had told her it was her only chance to keep racing. For two weeks after the operation, Juli couldn't put any weight on her left leg. Back home in Durango, Colorado, she spent the first weeks after surgery hopping around her new house, taking care of her dogs, and getting ready for her next big challenge. Recovering and strengthening her knee took her four months.

"You know, in a lot of ways, Juli will be stronger than ever when all is said and done," said Doug Martin. "Maybe for the first time in her entire career, she'll have two equally strong legs at work. When you consider everything Juli's accomplished already, that could be scary."

Ever since Juli was a child, she has loved to go fast.

Mountains in Her Blood

Juli has been interested in sports—and good at them—for as long as she can remember. If she had shown more of an interest in show business, no one would have been surprised. After all, both of her parents came from the world of arts and entertainment.

Juli was born in New York City on April 4, 1967. Her mother, Nina Armaugh, was a very fine ballet dancer before she got married and quit dancing to raise children. Juli's father, Tommy Furtado, was a cabaret singer. He became famous for singing at a popular nightclub in Manhattan. As a child, Juli took piano lessons and was a good musician too.

For many years, the Furtado family lived in suburban New Jersey, across the Hudson River from Manhattan. The third of four children, Juli shared the household with her older half brother Michael, her older sister Gia, and her younger brother Tommy.

Juli was a bike rider even as a toddler.

The Furtados lived in a suburb with clean air, tree-lined streets, light traffic, and plenty of parks. Juli, however, found ways to make life more exciting.

When Juli was just five, she was riding her bicycle back and forth across the street in front of her family's two-story house. When she swerved into the path of an oncoming car, the car knocked her to the ground. "I was so embarrassed, I didn't even want anybody to know what had happened," she says. "I was always very shy as a kid. So, I tried to pretend nothing had happened. I said I was OK, but I remember my hip really hurt."

Not long after that narrow escape, Juli wasn't quite so lucky. "I was eating lunch and watching my cat, who was sitting outside in front of the house," Juli remembers. "I went to check on her and suddenly she attacked me and chased me back into the house. I tried to slam the door, but I was too small and she was too fast. I had long hair then, and she climbed up my hair and tried to gouge my eyes. My parents got her off, then raced me to the hospital for stitches. I still have some scars. My own cat!"

A sports fan from the beginning, Juli spent her summers playing soccer and playing at the parks. Her best friend was a boy down the street who shared her interests. Juli enjoyed playing with her friends, but she didn't always enjoy going home.

Juli's mom, Nina, and her dad, Tommy, christened their second daughter Juliana.

Juli's parents had serious problems. Her mother grew bitter over giving up her dancing career. Her father, whose singing career often took him away from home, gradually became a heavy drinker. Her mother and father often had angry and explosive fights. Juli remembers it as a scary, violent time.

"My mom and dad were always fighting," she says, "physically as well as with words. One time, my mom locked my dad out of the house and told us that they were going to split up."

Juli was just seven years old when her parents decided to get a divorce. "My mom never had anything good to say about my dad," Juli says. "If one of us kids did something she didn't like, she'd say 'You're just like your father.' And we knew how she felt about him. Later, when he got remarried, she wouldn't let us go to the wedding."

Nina Furtado was determined to get away from where the family had lived. She packed up her three youngest children, rented a trailer, and moved 250 miles away. She took her children to Londonderry, Vermont, a small town near the Green Mountain National Forest. The Furtados had gone to Vermont on ski vacations in the past. It seemed as good a place as any to start over.

The comfortable, suburban life Juli and her brother and sister had known was gone. They lived in a creaky old farmhouse, which was heated by a wood-burning stove. The water pipes seemed to always be on the verge of bursting.

"We had tons of chores in that old house," says Juli. "We kept our expenses down by living simply. One winter the pipes finally went and we had to take baths at a neighbor's house down the road."

In order to make ends meet, Nina had to scramble. After spending much of her adult life as a dancer and full-time mother, she had no traditional job skills. But for years, she had dreamed of running her own ceramics shop, so she decided to do that. She used the front of the family house for the workshop and showroom. She called her shop "The Potter's Wheel." The store wasn't a great success, and it didn't make very much money for Juli's family.

"Those weren't great times," says Juli. "Everything seemed to be focused on money or the lack of money. We were constantly reminded of how broke we were. We pretty much survived on my dad's checks."

For Juli, community-sponsored recreation programs— soccer, baseball, and tennis—were her escape. One afternoon not long after they moved to Vermont, Juli's mother said she was going to enroll Juli in an after-school ski program. "She asked me if I wanted to ski **freestyle** or **alpine**," Juli said. "Thank god I said alpine."

Attracted by the speed and grace of the sport, Juli worked hard at learning to ski. With her natural talent and her hard work, she moved quickly from beginner to expert. Soon, she was one of the most promising young skiers in the area.

"I was such a dedicated kid," she says. "I'd stay out there all afternoon, half freezing to death, but I didn't care. I just kept going up and down, over and over again, trying to get better and better. No matter what I was doing, I always wanted to be the best I could possibly be."

Juli signed up for racing clinics and quickly improved. By the time she was 10, she was one of the best young skiers in the state. When she was 13, T. D. McCormick, a coach with area ski programs, took an interest in Juli. With his advice and support, she applied to the Stratton Mountain School, a respected private academy and ski school.

Ski coach T. D. McCormick helped Juli become an excellent skier.

Although she got cold, Juli never seemed to get tired of zooming down the ski slopes.

Juli attended Stratton Mountain School on a scholarship.

"T. D. helped me get sponsorships to cover expenses for equipment and entry fees," Juli recalls. "We didn't have much money, and scholarships to Stratton were very rare. I was just a kid. I didn't know what it took to pursue skiing. I just knew I loved the sport. T. D. put a lot of the pieces in place for me."

Stratton was filled with talented kids. But a youngster couldn't get in just because he or she could afford it. An applicant had to have good grades and be a talented skier, too. Also, Stratton didn't allow full-time students until ninth grade. For her first two years, Juli only attended during the winter term.

"I loved the academy, but I was always aware of being the poorest kid there, and that wasn't fun," Juli says. "On some trips, we'd drive right past my beat-up old house and I'd slink down in the car and pretend to be asleep."

Juli was an excellent student, and she eventually won a full scholarship to Stratton. That meant her family didn't have to pay for her schooling. Students who lived near Stratton were supposed to live at home while they went to school. But Juli moved into Stratton as a 10th grader.

For as long as she could remember, Juli had been fascinated by the Olympics. Her idol was American skier Tamara McKinney, an Olympian. Although she had just started training, Juli soon began winning against older, more experienced skiers. Her fantasy of skiing in the Olympics was starting to seem possible.

As a young skier, Juli wanted to be like U.S. Olympic skier Tamara McKinney, shown above.

At 16, Juli competed in the World Cup of skiing.

Dreams That
Live and Die

At Stratton Mountain School, Juli's life revolved around skiing for most of the year. Her schedule was demanding with schoolwork and training, but she put in the time and the effort to do well. As a student in the classroom, Juli never settled for anything lower than a B in her classes. She worked hard to keep up her grades. On the mountain, she never settled for less than first place. There, too, she had to work hard to reach her goals.

Under the watchful eye of Fritz Vallant, a former Austrian ski racer who coached at Stratton, Juli flourished. Vallant was demanding, but Juli respected him and wanted to please him. "He molded my skiing," she says. "He knew when to push me harder, when to just be supportive."

After long, difficult winters of skiing and schoolwork, Juli had little rest in the off-season. During the summer, she frequently went to training camps to keep in top physical condition. The camps usually lasted a couple of weeks. There were as many as 10 to 20 elite skiers at a camp. Sometimes campers were organized by age group, other times by event (slalom, downhill, **giant slalom**). Juli was often surrounded by classmates and skiers from Vermont.

"Those camps were fun, but they were also difficult," Juli says. "The daily schedules were incredibly busy. We'd ski all morning and then, after lunch, have **dryland training** all afternoon. When we weren't on the mountain, which was hard enough, we'd have to go through weightlifting sessions or play soccer, or do all kinds of other calisthenics exercises. We also did a lot of running."

With her natural love of speed and danger, Juli's knack for slalom and giant slalom quickly translated to victories. Slalom events are different from downhill. In slalom as in downhill, skiers have to rocket down the mountain as fast as they possibly can go. But in slalom, skiers must also twist and turn, zigzagging around a series of **gates** on the hillside. Slalom skiers try to beat three opponents: the clock, other skiers (who may be skiing beside them), and the natural challenges of the course itself. Each of these three problems, alone, can be trouble. Together, they make slalom skiing an extremely hazardous sport. But Juli was fearless, and that made her hard to beat.

Juli, far left, clowns around with some of her Stratton Mountain School classmates in her senior year.

When Juli was 14, she put herself in the international spotlight by finishing first in the world for her age group in time trials. In time trials, a skier races against the clock rather than against another skier. Time trials are used to determine which skiers will be chosen to go to big events, compete in important races, and earn a place on their country's national team. By winning her age group at the time trials, Juli proved she was a skier to watch.

Juli's excellent results would have earned her a spot on the U.S. National Ski Team that year, but she was too young. She continued to be an active unofficial member, training and traveling with the team.

Juli's natural talent, and her willingness to work hard, made her a terrific skier. She could fly down hills.

Throughout the following year, Juli continued to make news. With the 1984 Olympics just two years away, the 15-year-old was steadily knocking off the competition. Juli was trying for a chance to make the U.S. Olympic team that would go to Sarajevo. In 1982, she finished first in the world in her age group in slalom racing.

"I don't actually remember the exact moment when I found out I'd made the U.S. Team," she says. "I always knew it was just a matter of time. Still, it was an unbelievable thrill. I was the youngest skier on the team by three years and I was skiing side-by-side with Cindy Nelson and Kristin Cooper, two skiers I'd grown up watching and idolizing. When I got my team clothing—all the red, white, and blue outfits—it was just awesome."

That was also the year Juli earned the chance to compete in her first World Cup tournament. The World Cup of skiing is the most prestigious racing series in the sport. Skiers from around the world compete against each other not only for personal glory but for national pride as well. Only a few skiers earn spots on each country's team.

For Juli, skiing on the United States' World Cup team was the high point of her young skiing career. "It was so glamorous, so exciting," she says. "I was still just a kid, 16 years old, and competing in the pinnacle event of skiing. That year, the event was held in

Waterville, New Hampshire, which is close enough to where I grew up in Vermont that it felt like being at home. All my friends and family were there. My mom was a big supporter. It was a fantastic day. I didn't win or anything. I started near the back of the pack, and the course was rough and rutted by the time I took my run. But I had a really good time—on the clock, that is. That's all I wanted."

Just after her greatest year of skiing, Juli suffered her first major injury. And it didn't even happen during a race. In January of 1984, 16-year-old Juli returned home from a successful trip to Europe where she'd finished well in several events. With the 1984 Olympics approaching, Juli had only a short break before she would go to the U.S. national championships where the U.S. Olympic Team would be chosen.

During her break, Juli went to Bromley, Vermont, to watch a race. She spent the day with her best friend from Stratton, Colleen Quinn. Quinn had hurt her knee and was in a cast. After the race, Juli offered to carry her friend down the mountain.

"I remember how strange it was," Juli recalls. "I had Colleen on my back and everything was going fine. Then I crossed the tips of my skis and my **snowplow** went out of control. I didn't want to drop Colleen, so I struggled to keep my balance instead of just falling into the snow. Then I felt something in my left knee pop."

Juli's first injury happened on a ski slope, but not while she was skiing. She was hurt as she helped a friend down the hill.

"It hurt badly, but I acted like nothing happened. After all, here's poor Colleen with her leg in a cast. I went to the first aid center and told them I'd hurt my knee, but it was no big deal. We didn't do anything about it right away."

Juli's knee continued to hurt. Later in the week, she flew to California to have the U. S. Ski Team's surgeon, Dr. Richard Steadman, examine her.

"The knee joint was so loose," Juli says, "he could tell immediately that the ligament [which supports the joint] wasn't there any more. The next day, I had reconstructive surgery and after that I was laid up for a month. I watched the Olympics from my hospital bed. Needless to say, I was heartbroken."

After a month, the cast was removed from Juli's left leg and she began the long, painful task of rehabilitation. She spent hours rebuilding her strength. By the summer of 1984, Juli had successfully worked her way back to competing form.

Once doctors said Juli could ski again, she was sent by the U. S. Ski Team to Salt Lake City, Utah, for a week of dryland fitness training in July. After the dryland training, Juli would go to a ski camp in the mountains of South America. A former professional football player had been hired to lead the skiers in fitness exercises at the camp in Utah.

"It was awful," says Juli. "It was about 120 degrees every day. We worked so hard we'd get dizzy. He told us, 'I want you to work so hard you puke.' But if you did, he'd say the reason we were puking was we weren't in shape. And then he'd work us even harder. I think everybody cried at least once a day."

On the last day of camp, the trainees were ordered out onto the blistering artificial green for a drill. In this exercise, the athletes were directed to sprint full speed into a heavy bag, spin off, then sprint into the next one, spin off again, and so on until they finished the course. Juli lined up first and sprinted toward the first heavy bag, which was being held by the instructor.

"Just as I got to him, he must have leaned into the bag extra hard," Juli says, "because it felt like I got hit by a truck. I flew backward and landed really hard on my bad leg. Of course, the knee immediately blew out again. I knew it right away. I was crushed."

That afternoon, Juli flew back to California to see Dr. Steadman. The next day, she had the second major reconstruction operation on her left knee. "I think that was when I knew my chance of ever competing in the Olympics was basically gone," says Juli.

Juli's life had seemed carefree and charmed, but with another long recovery ahead of her, Juli was miserable. Could she stand another six months of rebuilding her knee? Could she bounce back from a whole year off and ever win?

By January of 1985, Juli had regained her strength and was healthy enough to ski again. She was racing well, showing no fear on the mountain, and keeping up with a hectic and challenging schedule. But late in the season, she hurt her knee once more. This time, surgeons installed Gortex strips to hold Juli's knee together. This operation was usually done on elderly people.

"Maybe I should have just quit right then and there," she says, "but I never even considered it. I was still really gung ho about getting back to the ski team. I was young. I thought I could still get there."

Her leg simply wasn't strong enough after a third operation. This time, the U.S. Ski Team sent her to Colorado. There, she raced at a lower level but still didn't do as well as she was used to doing. It was time for a change.

In the fall of 1986, Juli decided to take classes at the University of Colorado in Boulder. By then, she had also damaged her right knee. She had an 11-hole arthroscopy done on that knee. An arthroscopy is an operation in which a doctor looks at and sometimes repairs injured tissue through a small hole. Despite her injuries, Juli had the skill and strength to spend the next two years skiing for the University of Colorado, and she won some races.

During those two winters, Juli's left knee continued to get worse. The Gortex strip was unraveling. That meant that, sooner or later, she would have to have another operation to repair it.

Juli skied for the University of Colorado ski team.

With yet another major reconstruction operation ahead, Juli decided to quit skiing. The University of Colorado let her keep her scholarship for the next two years, even though she couldn't ski for the ski team. Juli figured that if she couldn't ski, she couldn't compete in the Olympics. Or could she?

37

After she quit skiing, Juli took up other sports.

The Road to Recovery

Despite her knee injuries, Juli continued to work out as hard as ever to gain strength and flexibility. Although her skiing career had ended, she wasn't about to give up all sports.

The summer after she quit skiing, Juli and some of her friends went to one of the final days of a bicycle **road race**. The race had started in San Francisco and was to end in Colorado after two weeks of daily **stage races**. Juli's friends knew some of the riders.

The next year, Juli signed up to work at the race. Her duties included keeping spectators off the course and watching the road for accidents and injuries. She was still hobbling after yet another knee operation and the hectic pace of the race was too demanding. After 10 days on the road, she left the race when the riders got to Colorado. But by then, she knew she wanted to try cycling.

Then Juli was introduced to another sport—the triathlon. In this strenuous three-part event, athletes swim, cycle, and run, all in the same day—sometimes in the same afternoon. The swim may be as short as a half-mile or as long as two miles. The bicycle race may cover up to 50 miles or more, at average speeds of more than 20 miles an hour. To finish, triathletes might run as many as 26 miles, the distance of a marathon.

Eager for new challenges, Juli began a training program and was soon signing up for competitions. "I loved to work as hard as I could," she says. "Triathlons seemed like a good idea. Even before I did my first one, I had signed up for a citizens' bike race in Vail, so at least the bike racing part wasn't totally foreign to me. I did OK in that race and, after that, I did my first triathlon. I was terrified. All I wanted was to finish. I'm a pretty bad swimmer, but I did well on the bike, and I was OK in the running part."

While finishing her business degree at school, Juli had to work to cover her living expenses. She took plenty of jobs to pay the bills, working as a hostess in a restaurant, as a bookkeeper, and at a bike shop.

"I didn't know anything about bikes at the time," Juli says. "I couldn't even fix a flat tire. I don't think it took too long for them to figure out I didn't know much. It was our little secret. But I learned a lot working there."

A natural athlete, Juli tried the three-sport triathlon.

Juli had been dabbling in triathlons and bicycle road racing for several summers. She hadn't been very serious about competing because school and work kept her busy. In the summer of 1989, Juli began to think about what to do after she graduated.

She decided to try bike racing. "I thought I'd spend the summer at it and see how well I could do if I was really committed," she says. Juli joined the Alfafa-Zen team, which was sponsored by a grocery store in Boulder. She traveled around the area, sometimes racing as often as twice a week while working at various jobs and studying.

Juli didn't win many races that summer, although she had some excellent finishes. Still, the experience taught her a lot about strategy. She knew she wasn't a good sprinter, so she learned to go out strong early in races. Late that summer, Juli went to the road nationals at Park City, Utah. Nearly 80 of the best women cyclists in the country gathered to crown a new champion of road cycling. A first-year racer, Juli figured she didn't have a chance of winning.

"I was definitely not the best racer there," she admits. "Laura Peycke and Ruthie Matthes were huge in road racing. I'd had a good summer, but these women were the best racers out there."

The course covered 15 laps of a hilly 3-mile circuit near Salt Lake City. As the race began, the July sun beat down on the riders. After the first lap, Juli was somewhat surprised to be near the front of the pack. "I've never been much of a sprinter," she says, "so I thought maybe I'd just go out and try to put some distance between myself and the rest of the pack. That's why I made a break and tried to sprint away from the field."

Breakaways are a common sight in road races. Usually, three, four, or five riders will sprint ahead of the main field, known as the peloton (pell-ah-TAHN). The breakaway riders try to take an early lead, which will help them in the closing moments of the race when the strongest racers often sprint to the finish. Often, the breakaway riders are not favorites to win the race, but they set a fast pace. Just as breakaways are common, it is also common for the peloton to bridge the gap between itself and the breakaway riders. To do so, the top riders in the peloton form a pace line, taking very short turns charging as hard as they can at the front of the pack. By **drafting,** or rotating from back to front with short bursts of speed, these riders can pull the entire group along at a very fast pace. The riders tuck into a long line with almost no space between each other and keep up a speed at which they eventually overtake the breakaway riders.

When Juli broke away from her group at Park City, no one in the group gave chase. Hers was a solo breakaway, the hardest to do. Juli was on her own, with no help.

After winning the 1989 road national championship, Juli went to the world competition in France.

The national championship was on the line. Juli decided to put her head down and pedal as hard as she could for as long as she could. Her training as a triathlete came in handy as she was able to keep up a smooth, blistering speed over the long day of racing. As the contest went on, Juli still expected the elite riders to come after her.

They never did. As she finished her final lap of the course, Juli had built a lead of nearly two minutes. When Juli crossed the finish line, she had done what nobody, including herself, thought possible. She had raced alone to a national championship in her first full season of racing.

"It was a total shock," she says. "To me and to everyone else. As a result of that win, I got to go to the world championships in France in September.

That was truly awesome. In France, I not only raced against the best American riders, but the best women riders in the world."

Juli didn't win at the world championships, but she raced well. Juli had established herself as a new star in cycling. But once again, her life took a major shift in direction.

"I was still in school at the time," she recalls, "and it was really important for me to graduate. Still, I had no idea what I was going to do when I got out of school. I had only picked business because I thought it would be a useful major. Suddenly, winning the road nationals, it occurred to me that maybe, just maybe, I could make a living as a bicycle racer."

Ruthie Matthes, left, and Juli relax after a tough ride.

5

Birth of a New Champion

After her upset victory at the 1989 U. S. Road Nationals, Juli began the 1990 bike racing season with enthusiasm and confidence. Halfway through the season, after careful thought, she switched from road racing to cross-country racing.

"In the end, it was a pretty easy decision," Juli says. "Because I wasn't a great sprinter, I knew I'd always struggle in road racing. It's hard to win road races if you can't finish strong. In cross-country, you use other skills, skills I thought were more in line with my strengths and weaknesses."

First, Juli had to find a new team and a new sponsor. She contacted John Parker, owner of Yeti Bicycles, and joined his Yeti racing team. She came close to winning several races before she went to the season-ending World Mountain Bike Championship in Durango, Colorado.

Climbing fast helps Juli in cross-country races.

"I was really nervous that day," she recalls. "I'd done a couple of road races there and I knew the terrain, but there were about 70 of the best riders in the world on hand, and it was a very demanding course."

The race began in Purgatory, nearly 7,500 feet above sea level. The course climbed more than 4,000 feet. It was a perfect course for Juli, who quickly jumped out to a lead and set a challenging pace. On the first big climb, she passed a number of the best riders by relying on her steady, unwavering rhythm. Juli says her exceptional lung capacity is what makes her able to climb so well.

"I can go one speed uphill for a long time without tiring out," she says. "I've always preferred long, steady climbs. At Purgatory, I had to be aggressive on the climbs because I was still kind of sketchy on the downhills. I was pretty out-of-control at times."

For the next two hours, Juli led the field around three laps of mountainous terrain. In the end, she built a two-minute lead over her friend and rival, Sara Ballantyne, and was strong enough to hold off any late challengers. Juli won the cross-country world championship in her first year of competition!

When the 1991 World Cup season began in Italy the following spring, Juli almost didn't go. She was close to finishing her business degree at the University of Colorado. She didn't want anything to interfere with her graduation from college. After Juli was able to adjust her school schedule, she went to Europe where she won the opening race of the Grundig UCI World Cup series and soon established herself as the series' top racer.

"I had a great year," she says. "I wore the [leader's] jersey all year—until the end, that is. The last race of the series was for double points and I had a terrible day. The race was in Berlin [Germany] and Sara Ballantyne beat me, took the extra points and I finished second in the World Cup points. It was a big disappointment."

Later that year, Juli won five of six races in the U. S. national Jeep cross-country series, an American-based pro circuit. Her only loss came to Ballantyne at Mammoth Mountain in California.

By 1992, Juli had switched to Team GT, which was based in California. In World Cup races, Juli had six top-three finishes and was runner-up to Ruthie Matthes. On the U. S. circuit, she won four of six races and took her second straight Jeep series title. All that was left for Juli was the challenging world championships at Bromont, Quebec. After a disappointing effort the previous year, Juli wanted to prove herself. But early in the race, she crashed and dislocated her left knee cap.

However, her weekend wasn't over. In qualifying for the downhill event, she had a flat tire. That put her dead last in the running order. She could barely bend her leg, but she attacked the difficult course.

"The best downhill riders were already done long before I got started," she says. "They were all waiting at the bottom when I started my run."

A crash early in the race ended Juli's hopes for a victory at the 1992 world championships in Bromont, Quebec.

The muddy challenge of cross-country racing attracts Juli.

"Then I went out and had the fastest time of the day and won. Wasn't I surprised!"

She wasn't the only one. After that performance, Juli's reputation for courage and skill became legendary. Racing experts encouraged her to focus on downhill events. Juli knew it would be nearly impossible to race downhill and cross-country. The two styles were too different. She felt her future was in cross-country. So, with one stunning victory under her belt, Juli left downhill racing.

In 1993, Juli was unbeatable. She entered nine World Cup races and won them all. Her past disappointments in Berlin were erased when she pulled off a dramatic come-from-behind victory for her first World Cup series title.

"I wanted to win so badly in Berlin," she says, "it just killed me. I was so nervous. All I needed was a seventh-place finish and I'd win the title. The course was a little park circuit, up and down the same hill over and over again. In the end, I was astonished to win. About 30 seconds into the race I dropped my chain. By the time I had it back in place, I was dead last. But I worked hard, rode smoothly, and got back to the front. It was exhausting and, at the end, they nearly caught me. I won by about five seconds. There was so much pressure on me to win that one."

In the 1993 Jeep series, Juli went six for six and won her third straight national title. She repeated the

World Cup and Jeep series double-win in 1994, winning 11 of 16 races and finishing second in two others. In the end, she was named the U. S. Cycling Federation's Female Athlete of the Year, the first mountain biker ever chosen for that honor.

In the 1994 world championships in Vail, Colorado, Juli ran out of energy and finished sixth. That led some people to say she "couldn't win the big one." After winning in 1990, Juli faced the expectation that she would win again and again.

"At Vail, I was devastated," she said. "I had won every race I entered that season and I was riding so well. But all week leading up to the race, I felt so tired. My legs were so beat up I could hardly walk."

Juli won her third World Cup series title with six victories and added her fifth Jeep series title in 1995. With the 1996 Olympic Games adding mountain bike racing as a medal sport, Juli also faced the challenge of qualifying for a spot on the women's team. She quickly won her spot with victories in two of the first four Olympic qualifying races.

In 1996, Juli won another qualifying race with a solid victory at the Olympic course in Conyers, Georgia. In World Cup competition, she finished second to Alison Sydor in three races before leaving the series to prepare for the Summer Games.

"I have to admit that in 1996, I didn't care about the World Cup or the U. S. national series," she says.

Juli just didn't have enough energy to win the 1994 title.

Although Juli loves to fly down hills, she concentrates on cross-country races in her professional career.

"All I really cared about was the Olympic Games. That had been my dream for so long."

The Olympics turned out to be a disappointment for Juli. She decided that her frustrating finish at the Olympics was just in keeping with a tough year. "It was a weird season," she says, "so Atlanta wasn't a total shock. I know I did everything I could to prepare. And it was a huge relief to have it over with."

Not long after, Juli went in for another arthroscopy. At that time, surgeons took a biopsy of her cartilage and grew it in the laboratory. In October, they reimplanted the cartilage and replaced her ligament. "It was definitely time to quit for the year," she says. "I couldn't have raced much longer. My knee was pretty much destroyed by then."

In January of 1997, recuperating from her latest knee operation, Juli traveled to California to prepare for another season of World Cup and U. S. cross-country racing. But her physical troubles continued. She became sick with a fever and swollen joints. Her illness was diagnosed as Lyme disease, a bacterial infection carried by deer ticks.

Juli didn't let the disease stand in the way of her comeback. In her first race of 1997, the Grundig UCI World Cup opener at Napa Valley, California, she finished 13th. But anyone who knows Juli and knows her many comebacks, knows she won't be satisfied until she is first once more.

With all her injuries, can Juli soar once more?

Career Highlights

- Won World Mountain Bike Championship, 1990, 1992
- Named to U.S. World Mountain Bike Team, 1990–95
- Took second at the 1995 Pan American Games, 1995
- Won Jeep Cross-Country Series National Championship, 1993, 1994, 1995
- Won Grundig/UCI World Cup Series Championship, 1993, 1994, 1995
- Named Female Cyclist of the Year by *VeloNews,* 1995
- Named Female Athlete of the Year by the U.S. Cycling Federation, 1994
- Named International Cyclist of the Year by *VeloNews,* 1993
- Qualified for World Mount Bike Championships in 1990–95
- Won five of the seven U.S. Olympic qualifying events, 1995–96
- Won U.S. Road Race cycling championship, 1989
- Named to the U.S. Olympic Ski Team, 1980–87

Glossary

alpine: A type of skiing in which the skier slides down a steep slope.

anaerobic: Without oxygen. Anaerobic exercises are usually done in short bursts.

anterior cruciate ligament: A tough band of tissue within the center of the knee that connects bones.

cross-country: A competition that is through the countryside, rather than on a track. There are cross-country races in bicycling and skiing.

downhill: A race in which competitors try to be the first one down a steep slope or hill. There are downhill races in bicycling and skiing.

drafting: A technique in which a competitor stays just behind another to reduce the wind resistance he or she must face.

dryland training: Exercises that are done on the ground or in a gym, and that help athletes practice the moves they will use on the snow.

freestyle: A competition in which entrants are allowed to use a variety of techniques and styles. There are freestyle races in skiing and swimming.

gates: The obstacles racers must go between on a slalom course.

giant slalom: A race in which competitors may choose their own path between obstacles while going downhill.

Juli shows strength and power in a cross-country race.

road race: A race in which competitors ride on a path or road, rather than on a designated track.

slalom: A race in which competitors must weave between obstacles while going downhill. There are slalom races in bicycling and skiing.

snowplow: A skiing move in which the skier slides downhill slowly with the tips of the skis pointing in and the ends pointing out.

stage races: Individual parts of a longer race. There are breaks between stage races.

61

Sources

Information for this book was obtained from the following sources: interviews with Juli Furtado, Doug Martin, and Dr. Wayne Gersoff; *The New York Times Magazine*, 23 June 1996; Geoff Drake, *Bicycling*, May 1994; Scott Martin, *Bicycling*, May 1996; *Ski*, May/June, 1995; Sara Corbett, *Outside*, August 1995; Diane Loupe, *Atlanta Journal-Constitution*, 30 July 1996.

Index

Write to Juli:

You can send mail to Juli at the address on the right. If you write a letter, don't get your hopes up too high. Juli and other athletes get lots of letters every day, and they aren't always able to answer them all.

Juli Furtado
c/o Team GT
3100 West Segerstrom Avenue
Santa Ana, CA 92704

Acknowledgments

Photos are reproduced with the permission of: pp. 1, 61, Neil Palumbo/Bliss Images USA; pp. 2, 38, 45, 55, © Jim Safford/ Photosport; pp. 6, 14, 48, 51, 52, © Tom Moran/Singletrack; p. 9, Mac Weist/Image Bureau; pp. 10, 58, © Casey B. Gibson; p. 13, © ALLSPORT USA/Nathan Bilow; pp. 16, 18, 19, 26, 41, Juli Furtado; pp. 22, 29, © Hubert Schriebl; pp. 23, 30, 33, Sports File/Jerry LeBlond; p. 24, © Stratton Mountain School; p. 25, © ALLSPORT USA; p. 37, Courtesy of University of Colorado Athletic Media Relations; p. 44, © Cor Vos; p. 46, © David Epperson; p. 56, Malcolm Fearon/Bliss Images USA; p. 62, Hiroyuki Kaijo/Bliss Images USA.

Front cover photographs by (top and right) © Rich Etchberger and (left) Neil Palumbo/Bliss Images USA. Back cover photograph by © Gunnar Conrad.

Artwork by John Erste.

About the Author

Morgan Hughes is the author of two other sports biographies for young readers. A freelance writer, Morgan lives with his family in Pennsylvania.